Bible Chapters for Kids

My Shepherd

© 2015 iCharacter Ltd.

The Lord is my loving shepherd. He gives me what I need.

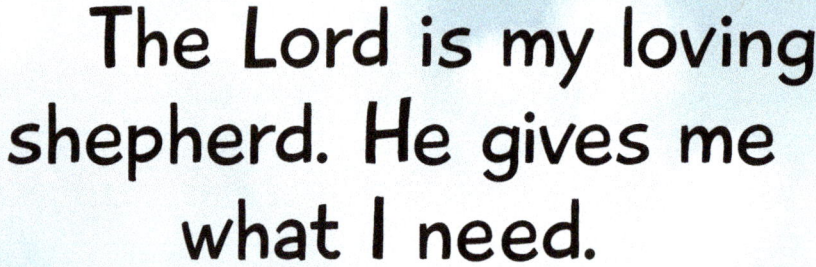

"The Lord is my shepherd;
I shall not want."

He blesses me with a place to rest.

"He maketh me to lie down in green pastures;"

He gives me peace.

"He leadeth me beside the still waters."

He gives strength
to my spirit.

"He restoreth my soul;"

He helps me do what is right, so that others will see how good the Lord is.

"He leadeth me in paths of righteousness for his name's sake."

So, even when things look dark and scary ...

"Yea, though I walk through the valley of the shadow of death,"

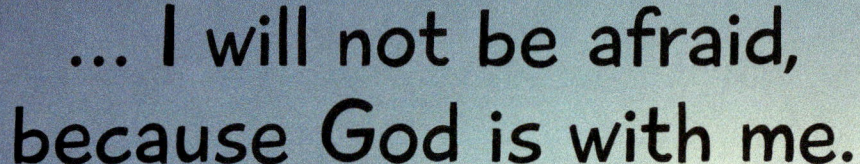

... I will not be afraid, because God is with me.

He protects me and brings me comfort.

"Thy rod and thy staff, they comfort me."

God welcomes me with his love. I overflow with his blessings.

"Thou anointest my head with oil; my cup runneth over."

His goodness and love will always be there for me.

"Surely goodness and mercy shall follow me all the days of my life;"

And I will live with him forever, here and in heaven.

"And I will dwell in the house of the Lord forever."

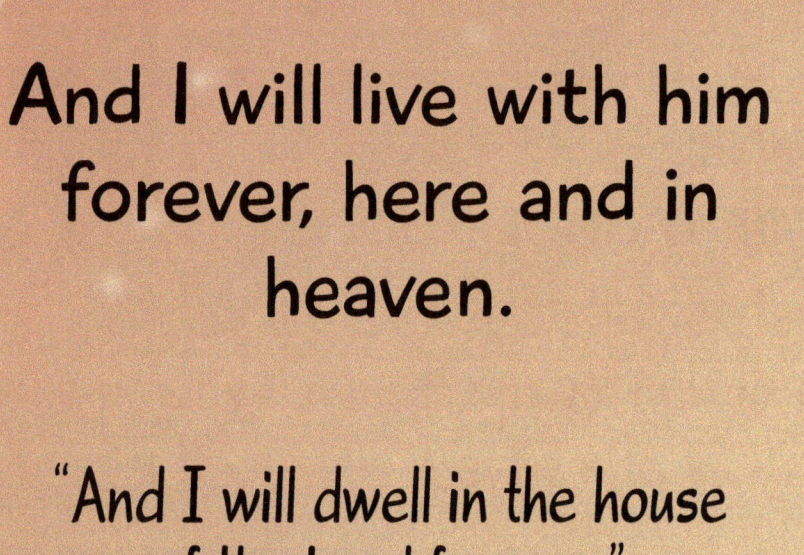

Help the shepherd find his lost sheep.

Use these pictures to tell the story of how the good shepherd cares for his sheep.

Can you find these pictures somewhere in the book?

Find the 8 differences.

The Lord is my shepherd; I shall not want.
He maketh me to lie down in green pastures:
he leadeth me beside the still waters.
He restoreth my soul: he leadeth me in the paths of
righteousness for his name's sake.
Yea, though I walk through the valley of the shadow of
death, I will fear no evil: for thou art with me;
thy rod and thy staff they comfort me.
Thou preparest a table before me in the presence of
mine enemies: thou anointest my head with oil;
my cup runneth over.
Surely goodness and mercy shall follow me all the days of
my life: and I will dwell in the house of the Lord for ever.

More books in the series:

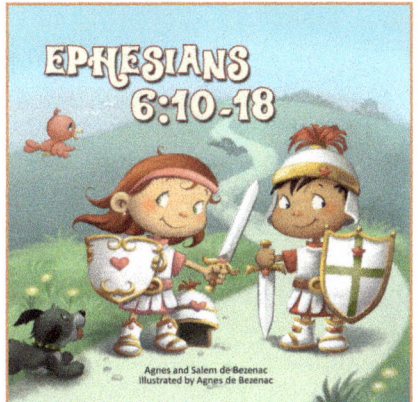

 Please help spread the word by introducing your friends to our products.

 Visit our website at iCharacter.org.
www.icharacter.org

 You can also get our books from the iBookstore, Kobo, Amazon Kindle, Google Play and B&N.

 Follow us on Facebook.
www.facebook.com/icharacter

 See us on YouTube.
www.youtube.com/ichactervideos

 Follow us on Twitter to stay updated: @icharacternews
www.twitter.com/icharacternews

Published by iCharacter Ltd. (Ireland)
www.icharacter.org
By Agnes and Salem de Bezenac
Illustrated by Agnes de Bezenac
Colored by Henny Y.
Copyright 2015. All rights reserved.
All Bible verses adapted from the KJV.

Copyright © 2012 by Agnes and Salem de Bezenac. All rights reserved. No part of this book may be reproduced in any form or by any electronic or mechanical means, including information storage and retrieval systems, without written permission from the publisher or author, except in the case of a reviewer, who may quote brief passages embodied in critical articles or in a review.

www.ingramcontent.com/pod-product-compliance
Lightning Source LLC
LaVergne TN
LVHW072053060526
838200LV00061B/4727